Strategic Studies Institute Monograph

MEXICO'S "NARCO-REFUGEES": THE LOOMING CHALLENGE FOR U.S. NATIONAL SECURITY

Paul Rexton Kan

I0447431

October 2011

*****

Comments pertaining to this report are invited and should be forwarded to: Director, Strategic Studies Institute, U.S. Army War College, 632 Wright Ave, Carlisle, PA 17013-5046.

*****

All Strategic Studies Institute (SSI) publications may be downloaded free of charge from the SSI website. Hard copies of this report may also be obtained free of charge while supplies last by placing an order on the SSI website. The SSI website address is: *www.StrategicStudiesInstitute.army.mil.*

*****

The Strategic Studies Institute publishes a monthly e-mail newsletter to update the national security community on the research of our analysts, recent and forthcoming publications, and upcoming conferences sponsored by the Institute. Each newsletter also provides a strategic commentary by one of our research analysts. If you are interested in receiving this newsletter, please subscribe on the SSI website at *www.StrategicStudiesInstitute. army.mil/newsletter/.*

FOREWORD

The security and stability of America's southern neighbor has been a condition taken for granted by many U.S. policymakers. While the U.S. defense establishment, in particular, has been focused on wars in Iraq and Afghanistan, the potential for spillover violence from Mexico cannot be dismissed. Over 30,000 Mexicans have been killed since Mexican President Felipe Calderon launched a campaign to destroy drug cartels and gangs, which have perpetrated heinous acts of violence like dismemberments and decapitations. Small towns in Mexico near the U.S. border have been abandoned out of fear of criminal violence. Businesses have reconsidered their investments and their operations in Mexico.

Such large-scale violence in other countries has led many people to seek safety by crossing an international border. This is beginning to happen with Mexicans seeking asylum in the United States. Dr. Kan examines the growing movement of Mexicans who are coming to the United States out of fear of cartel violence. Unlike illegal immigration, these Mexicans are leaving unwillingly. The effects of such a movement, if it increases steadily or suddenly, will force U.S. policymakers to rethink much of the strategic environment in the hemisphere and place pressure on them to reconsider national security priorities. The effects will also be felt in U.S. domestic political debates over immigration, public safety, and border security.

DOUGLAS C. LOVELACE, JR.
Director
Strategic Studies Institute

ABOUT THE AUTHOR

PAUL REXTON KAN is Associate Professor of National Security Studies and the holder of the Henry L. Stimson Chair of Military Studies at the U.S. Army War College. In February 2011, he served as the Senior Visiting Counternarcotics Adviser at North Atlantic Treaty Organization Headquarters in Kabul, Afghanistan. He recently completed field research along the U.S.-Mexico border for this monograph and for his upcoming book, *Cartels at War: Understanding Mexico's Drug-Fueled Violence and the Challenge to U.S. National Security*. Dr. Kan is the author of *Drugs and Contemporary Warfare* and numerous articles on the intersection of drug trafficking, crime, and modern forms of armed conflict including: "Drugging Babylon: The Illegal Narcotics Trade and Nation-Building in Iraq"; "'Lawyers, Guns and Money': Transnational Threats and U.S. National Security"; and "Criminal Sovereignty: Understanding North Korea's Illicit International Activities."

SUMMARY

Since 2006, when Mexican president Felipe Calderon declared war on the drug cartels, there has been a rise in the number of Mexican nationals seeking political asylum in the United States to escape the ongoing drug cartel violence in their home country. Political asylum cases in general are claimed by those who are targeted for their political beliefs or ethnicity in countries that are repressive or failing. Mexico is neither. Nonetheless, if the health of the Mexican state declines because criminal violence continues, increases, or spreads, U.S. communities will feel an even greater burden on their systems of public safety and public health from "narco-refugees." Given the ever-increasing brutality of the cartels, the question is whether and how the United States Government should begin to prepare for what could be a new wave of migrants coming from Mexico.

Allowing Mexicans to claim asylum could potentially open a floodgate of migrants to the United States during a time when there is a very contentious national debate over U.S. immigration laws pertaining to illegal immigrants. On the other hand, to deny the claims of asylum seekers and return them to Mexico, where they might very well be killed, strikes at the heart of American values of justice and humanitarianism. This monograph focuses on the asylum claims of Mexicans who *unwillingly* leave Mexico, rather than those who willingly enter the United States legally or illegally. To navigate wisely in this sea of complexity will require greater understanding and vigilance at all levels of the U.S. Government.

MEXICO'S "NARCO-REFUGEES": THE LOOMING CHALLENGE FOR U.S. NATIONAL SECURITY

The word for "border" in English and Spanish reveals a philosophical divide. While in English, "border" connotes a boundary that delineates a fixed separation that can serve as a barrier to the outside, in Spanish the word is "frontera" which can also mean "frontier" — or the beginning of a new territory. In Mexico's colloquial Spanish, "the border" is often called "la linea," or "the line," which implies something arbitrarily drawn by a subjective hand. Indeed, many leaving Mexico today see the area beyond the northern frontier as a zone of relative safety, a crossing of the line in the hope of finding peace that is elusive at home because of drug cartel and gang violence. They are "narco-refugees."

The ongoing drug cartel violence in Mexico took a very worrisome turn in April 2010. While the killings of two American consular employees in Juarez were a serious escalation, even more troubling was the motivation behind an event that took place several miles away and several days later. Thirty people of the small Mexican town of El Porvenir walked the 860 yards to the border and went to the small Texas town of Fort Hancock to seek political asylum from an explicit cartel threat. The threat was as simple as it was cruel: leave before the outbreak of a gang war or else your children will be targets . . . unless you provide $350 in pesos per child for protection.[1] The gang was able to purge the town of human obstacles and earn money for weapons from those who could afford to pay the extortion money.

1

Since 2006, when Mexican president Felipe Calderon declared war on the drug cartels, there has been a rise in the number of Mexican nationals seeking political asylum in the United States to escape the ongoing drug cartel violence in their home country. In 2008, 312 Mexicans lodged formal asylum requests when they arrived at the U.S. border, and another 2,231 asked for asylum in 2008 after entering the United States.[2] While the numbers appear small, these numbers are up from 179 in 2007 and just 54 in 2006. Strikingly, no Mexicans asked for asylum in the 1990s during that decade's brief but bloody outbreak of drug cartel violence.[3] The actual number of narco-refugees is likely higher, because many others have fled and have chosen to live discreetly without formally requesting asylum in the United States. Some Mexican analysts have estimated that as many as 200,000 people may have fled just Ciudad Juarez for other parts of Mexico or the United States.[4] Of that number, according to the Ciudad Juarez Citizens Security and Coexistence Observatory, about 124,000 people may have sought safe haven in El Paso.[5] These numbers do not reflect the total number of asylum claims, but likely do reflect those Mexicans who are using B1/B2 Visas, which allow them to temporarily visit the United States for a specified length of time and who are now using the visas to live temporarily on the U.S. side of the border. These so-called "*inversionistas*" work in Mexico during the day, but come to the United States at night, when the violence is at its worst back home.[6] Yet, the rise in formal pleas for asylum is occurring as the numbers of illegal immigrants from Mexico are *declining*, according to the U.S. Border Patrol — pointing to a troubling trend in the reasons for Mexicans coming northward.[7]

Political asylum cases in general are claimed by those who are targeted for their political beliefs or ethnicity in countries that are repressive or failing. Mexico is neither, and those who are being targeted by cartels and gangs are police who investigate crimes; mayors who govern towns; journalists who write about the violence; businessmen who could be kidnapped for ransom; and ordinary citizens who are in the way. Nonetheless, when people involuntarily leave their home country *en masse* for another, it is one sign that the home government is weakening and that the health of a state is being compromised. With a population of over 100 million, Mexico and the health of its state are of acute concern to the United States.

If the health of the Mexican state declines because criminal violence continues, increases, or spreads, U.S. communities will feel an even greater burden on their systems of public safety and public health from narco-refugees. Given the ever-increasing brutality of the cartels, the question is whether and how the U.S. Government should begin to prepare for what could be a new wave of migrants coming from Mexico. As former U.S. attorney Pete Nunez said, "What happens on one side [of the border] quite often affects what happens on the other side."[8]

Yet, the lack of a clear U.S. policy on what to do about narco-refugees from Mexico mirrors the complicated U.S. relationship with Mexico itself, thus compounding the complication. Mexico is a large trading partner of the United States, and the current Mexican government's actions against the cartels have received widespread support from American policymakers. To admit an increasing number of asylum seekers into the United States undermines the message that Mexico is safe for American businesses and that the Mexican government is strong enough to prevail against the cartels. Also, allowing Mexicans to claim asylum could potentially open a floodgate of migrants to the United States during a time when there is a very contentious national debate over U.S. immigration laws pertaining to illegal immigrants. On the other hand, to deny the claims of asylum seekers and return them to Mexico where they might very well be killed strikes at the heart of American values of justice and humanitarianism. To navigate successfully in this sea of complexity will require greater understanding and vigilance at all levels of the U.S. Government.

This monograph focuses on the asylum claims of Mexicans who *unwillingly* leave Mexico, rather than those who willingly enter the United States legally or illegally. The most recent cases of mass migration of asylum seekers to the United States were the Mariel Boat Lift in 1980, the Haitian exodus in the early 1990s, and an influx of Cuban rafters, also in the early 1990s. Each of these episodes was the result of civil unrest under repressive regimes, and the exoduses occurred at sea. Nonetheless, they began suddenly and created political and foreign policy challenges for decision-makers. In Mexico, the violence that has surrounded competition over key areas in drug trafficking networks has frequently produced mass movements of people across borders in other cases—whether it be Colombia and Peru from the 1980s through the 1990s or Burma in the 1990s. The possibility of a mass migration of narco-refugees from Mexico over a land border may create an exponentially growing number of challenges for U.S. decisionmakers and may even present new tests for U.S. national security.

"WE ARE NOT USED TO THIS TYPE OF VIOLENCE. THE HEADS"[9]

In his book, *The Three US-Mexico Border Wars*, Tony Payan warns against conflating the war against illegal immigration with the War on Drugs and the War on Terror: "Each problem has its own dynamics, its own actors, its own motives, its own scenarios — even when there are points of intersection among them. Bluntly put, they are not the same issue, and they should not be treated as such."[10] But the war *inside* Mexico — the war of the cartels against each other and their war against the government — is now contributing to the conflation. The violence of drug trafficking organizations is terrorizing people into migrating. This reinforces certain broad historical narratives of the region's criminal traditions.

Lawlessness south of the U.S.-Mexico border is nothing new. A culture of crime and banditry has long existed throughout the northern Mexican states and the Southwestern United States; this culture benefited from geographical homogeneity, terrain favorable to criminal activities, impoverished communities easily attracted to enrichment through nefarious means, and a folklore mentality that celebrates the exploits of larger-than-life characters existing outside the law.[11]

Charles Bowden, a long-time journalist who has chronicled the social issues on the U.S.-Mexico border, reflects how contemporary criminal activities are leading to a disintegration of familiar and comfortable patterns of life in the region:

> One city is called El Paso, the other Juarez. One state is called Texas, the other Chihuahua. One nation is called the United States, the other Mexico. I find it harder

and harder to use these names because they imply order and boundaries, and both are breaking down. So I stumble and try not to say these names even though they have meaning left, and they are right there on the maps and road signs. But they have the feel of the past, of dust and ruin and dead dreams. And so I say them at times, but often I struggle to find a way around these words because uttering them or writing them down contributes to a big lie and helps trap people in a dying world.[12]

In many respects, the border has always been a blurry space, rather than a bright defining line that has separated two sides. The blurriness serves as a rich ecology for criminality. Mexico has a history of supplying the longstanding American appetite for illicit substances, from *tequileros* who smuggled liquor into the United States during Prohibition to today's *maras* (gangs) who move narcotics along familiar routes of past illicit activity. Mexico suffers from a "location curse," because it lies between drug suppliers and the U.S. market.[13] Border cities such as Nuevo Laredo, Juarez, and Tijuana have a strategic location in the drug trade and consequently have witnessed intense fighting. The cartels and gangs are struggling for control over "strategic warehouses" and smuggling routes, known as *plazas*, which provide easy access into the United States.[14] The location curse supports a common Mexican saying: "Pobre Mexico. Tan lejos de Dios; tan cerca de los Estados Unidos" ("Poor Mexico. So far from God; so close to the United States").

But location is only one of the curses afflicting Mexico; the violence that it is suffering is gruesome in its manifestations and staggering in it proportions. Since 2006, more than 28,000 Mexicans have been murdered, and Mexico now ranks first in the Americas region for kidnappings. So pervasive is the cruelty of the cartels that a unique lexicon has emerged to describe the crimes:

- Decapitado: decapitation
- Descuartizado: quartering of a body, carving it up
- Encuelado: body in trunk of car
- Encobijado: body wrapped in blanket
- Entampado: body in a drum
- Enteipado: eyes and mouth of corpse taped shut
- Pozoleado (also Guisado): body dissolved in acid, looking like Mexican stew.[15]

Several areas in Mexico are experiencing civil violence or "large scale violence [that] generates desperation, as people take extraordinary steps to attack persons or property ordinarily left in peace, or to avoid becoming victims of such attacks. Under these circumstances, all bets are off on a wide variety of normal social interactions."[16] Civil violence in Mexico defies easy classification—is it insurgency, terrorism, gangsterism, or all of them combined? General Barry McCaffrey (retired), former head of the Office of National Drug Control Policy, asserts that Mexico is experiencing "narco-terrorism."[17] Meanwhile, Hal Brands has called Mexican violence a "multisided narco-insurgency."[18] Secretary of State Hillary Clinton described Mexico as an "insurgency" that is "looking more and more like Colombia looked 20 years ago."[19] Phil Williams and I borrow the term "high-intensity crime."[20] Robert Bunker and John Sullivan have dubbed the violence "criminal insurgency."[21] Mexicans generally refer to the situation as "La Inseguridad" (The Insecurity).

How the violence is described affects how the United States might treat those who are leaving Mexico. If the violence is more akin to an internal war, then "refugee" becomes a more practical term. But if the violence is criminal in nature, the legal path to asylum becomes much more complicated. If the violence is some combination of war and crime, "somewhere between Al Capone's Chicago and an outright war,"[22] the murkiness may also impede those seeking legal sanctuary in the United States.

REFUGEES AND POLITICAL ASYLUM— CAUGHT IN THE PROBLEM, CAUGHT IN THE SOLUTION

The proximity of the United States is both the fuel for the civil violence in Mexico and the possible refuge from it. An advertisement in a Spanish language San Diego magazine asks, "Feeling Unsafe?" The ad targets Tijuana families who are seeking to escape the drug violence, with the advertiser offering services to help find homes to buy or rent in San Diego plus assistance with visas, border-crossing documents, and even help to enroll children in American schools.[23] Due to the number of home invasions and kidnappings among Mexicans in the United States, another company, Puertas Multilock, advertises security doors on the web in Spanish for "the confidence and protection of your home."[24] These are businesses specifically conceived to capitalize on the spillover effects of cartel violence.

The publisher of Mexico's most influential newspaper, Alejandro Junco, moved his family from Monterrey, Mexico, to Texas after he was threatened and gunmen paid a visit to his ranch. Other businessmen from cities across Mexico have done the same.[25] Mr. Junco now commutes every week to Mexico from Texas.[26] In fact, he has publicly called himself a "refugee."[27] Many professionals from both the private and public sectors in Mexico are leaving to find sanctuary in the United States. Several mayors from Mexico's northern border states of Tamaulipas, Chihuahua, and Nuevo Leon have moved to the United States, with some taking up residence permanently and others splitting their time between U.S. and Mexican residences.[28] Private and public professionals can afford to start new lives in the United States, but many other Mexicans cannot and have sought formal asylum.

In order to claim political asylum, one must first be a refugee. The definition of a refugee within U.S. jurisprudence is:

> Any person who is outside any country of such person's nationality or, in the case of a person having no nationality, is outside any country in which such person last habitually resided, and who is unable or unwilling to return to, and is unable or unwilling to avail himself or herself of the protection of, that country because of persecution or well-founded fear of persecution on account of race, religion, nationality, membership in a particular social group, or political opinion.[29]

An applicant must demonstrate that past persecution occurred and will likely recur if he or she is repatriated, and that such persecution is due to at least one of the five criteria established in the definition above (race, religion, nationality, membership in a particular social group, or political opinion). Another part of the definition is that persecution was committed or that future persecution would be committed by the government, nongovernment actors with the acquiescence of the government, or a group that the government is unable or unwilling to control.[30]

All of these facets form a high legal threshold for asylum eligibility, which appears nearly unreachable for many Mexicans. The total number of asylum claims is notoriously difficult to track, due to their confidentiality, but in 2008, only 13 percent of asylum claims for Mexicans were granted. It is unknown whether any of these included individuals who fled cartel violence.[31] That many Mexicans in the United States are fearful of returning because of retribution is beyond dispute. In a sampling of narco-refugees who have spoken to the press, accounts of violence are comparable to those of many wartime atrocities.

- The niece of a former police commander claims, "I am afraid for my life and for the lives of my children." Her uncle's head was found in a sack with eight other heads of police officers.[32]
- A Mexican boy from El Porvenir witnessed his mother, grandfather, aunt, and uncle tortured with ice picks.[33]
- Before leaving Mexico, witnesses to cartel crimes had their houses burned down in several areas of the Juarez Valley.[34]
- Alejandro Hernandez Pacheco, the cameraman for the Televisa network, said, "[The kidnappers] hung us on a cross. I'm proud to be Mexican, but you can't work under those conditions, and I'm scared."[35]

Those who have fled included state agents like mayors and police officers, as well as those related to them. Astonishingly, a total of 915 municipal police, 698 state police, and 463 federal agents have been killed.[36]

But members of civil society like journalists have been at increasing risk. According to the International Press Institute, which tracks crimes against members of the news media, Mexico is the most dangerous country in Latin America for journalists.[37] Wealthy businessmen and salaried professionals like teachers, as well as their relatives, have been kidnapped for ransom and compelled to name others who they believe might be worth kidnapping. Witnesses to cartel crimes are subject to intimidation and, as in the case of El Porvenir, those who are merely in the way of an impending gang fight are under threat and have decided to leave.

But are they being persecuted because they belong to any of the five categories laid out by the Immigration and Nationality Act (INA) Section 101(a)(42)(A)? This is a question that courts and the Board of Immigration Appeals (BIA) have been generally reluctant to answer in the affirmative. This approach has led to cries that "[the U.S.] Government's interpretation of the law is going to cause people to die."[38] In the case of a Mexican police informant, Guillermo Eduardo Ramirez-Peyro, his attorneys argued successfully in front of the Eighth Circuit Court of Appeals that asylum could be granted, not based on INA Section 101, but on the United Nations (UN) Convention Against Torture that the United States signed in 1988.[39] "The court said that under the convention, 'acquiescence by government officials that could lead to a petitioner's harm' was grounds to grant political asylum."[40] The case of Ramirez-Peyro is unique as well as controversial. Known also as "Lalo," he was a paid informant of U.S. Immigration and Customs Enforcement (ICE) and was tainted by allegations that he carried out several killings for the Juarez cartel, including during his time as an informant.[41] Even as a government asset, he spent over 5 years in detention while he awaited the final disposition of his case. This raises another relevant issue — enduring the asylum process is not easy.

Generally, asylum applications are made at a U.S. port of entry. When the application is made at a port of entry, a Customs and Border Protection (CBP) officer conducts a preliminary investigation to determine whether the alleged fear of persecution is credible. The threshold is very low at a port of entry, because the officers prefer to err on the side of caution. The applicant is then transferred to a detention facility managed by the ICE Detention and Removal Office (DRO). The applicant remains in the detention facility until an Asylum Officer travels there for a full credible-fear interview. While awaiting the Asylum Officer's decision, applicants can request to be released on parole (and granted a special permit known as Temporary Protected Status) and may even request employment authorization. An Employment Authorization Document (also known as an EAD Card) enables them to legally obtain employment while they are in the United States. EAD cards will generally be approved, because the government does not want the applicants to be present here as a "public charge." Before December 2009, asylum seekers were detained while their applications were processed, therefore many evaded the legal avenues of redress and lived like other illegal migrants. Since 2010, the Obama administration has permitted them to enter the United States while their claims are processed.

However, if the asylum application is believed to be based on phony information, parole will be denied. Upon denial of the asylum application, the person can still file an appeal with an Immigration Judge (IJ) who works for the Department of Justice (DOJ), not for the Department of Homeland Security (DHS) like U.S. Customs personnel do. A full hearing with legal representation and witnesses is held. If the IJ overturns the denial, the person is granted asylum and released. If the IJ affirms the denial, the person can still file an appeal with the BIA, and later with the Circuit Court, and all the way to the Supreme Court.

U.S. Citizenship and Immigration Service (USCIS), another component of DHS, gets involved when a person is already in the United States, either legally or illegally. While in the United States, asylum seekers must file applications with USCIS within 1 year of entry. The USCIS asylum officers then decide the case. If the application is approved, the asylum seeker is then given a Lawfully Admitted for Permanent Residence (LAPR [pronounced Lapper]) Card, more familiarly known as a green card. If the application is denied, the person is issued a voluntary departure letter with a specific date for departure from the United States. A copy of the letter is sent to ICE DRO for follow-up if the person does not depart voluntarily. While waiting to depart, the applicant can file a new application for asylum with an IJ (because the individual is now in removal proceedings). The appeal process is the same as detailed above. If the judge rejects the case, there is a high likelihood that the applicant will be deported. The lengthy process, together with unspecified duration of detention, while difficult to endure, may act as a type of filtering process to sort out legitimate claims from illegitimate ones. Some simply give up on the process and return to Mexico to take their chances. With drug cartels and gangs increasingly expanding into immigrant smuggling, other Mexicans may have been forced into the ironic position of seeking them out so that they can be smuggled into the United States as a way to escape the cartels and gangs.

Yet, the process reveals that those who seek asylum are not only caught in the brutal drug violence, but in the U.S. security and immigration process. When it comes to entering the United States from abroad, the U.S. Government has focused on strengthening border security and immigration enforcement, especially since September 11, 2001 (9/11). Some of the key pieces have been:

- Tightening of terrorism laws and expansion of investigative authorities to reduce the risk in the immigrant and nonimmigrant admissions process.
- Toughening of the visa, admission, and travel screening procedures at consulates, airports, and ports of entry.
- Reinforcement of border security through the expansion of the Border Patrol, especially at the southern border with Mexico, and by the Coast Guard in maritime channels.[42]

These key pieces combine to stymie many Mexican asylum cases. Are they genuine claims, or are they invented as another way for Mexicans to enter the United States in pursuit of other goals? A complicating factor in substantiating claims is the emergence of "narco-censorship," in which Mexican "reporters and editors, out of fear or caution, are forced to write what the traffickers want them to write, or to simply refrain from publishing the whole truth in a country where members of the press have been intimidated, kidnapped, and killed."[43] As previously mentioned, a cameraman from a national TV station, Televisa, who was kidnapped by members of the Sinaloa drug cartel and then released, has sought political asylum in the United States.[44] The goal of attacking the media is to reduce the news coverage to make Mexican civil society less aware of the activities of the cartels and gangs, thus keeping people less able to form accurate opinions and act against the groups.[45] This campaign of coercion appears to be working. In September 2010, the editors of the major newspaper in Ciudad Juarez offered a truce with the drug cartels:

> To the organizations that are disputing the plaza of Ciudad Juarez: the loss of two reporters of this publishing house in less than 2 years represents an irreparable breakdown for all of us who work here and, in particular, for their families. We would like it to be known, we are communicators, not psychics. With that in mind, as information correspondents, we want you to explain, What is it you want from us? What is it you want us to publish, or stop publishing? Explain so we can attend these issues.

> You are, at present, the de facto authorities of this city. . . . This is not a surrender. Nor does it mean we will give up on the work we have been developing. This is a respite, an offering of truce to those who have imposed their law on this city, providing they respect the lives of those of us who dedicate ourselves to informing the public.[46]

Such a "truce," and self-censorship more broadly, will have a deleterious effect on narco-refugees — there will be less evidence to corroborate their stories. This will leave asylum officers and immigration judges at a disadvantage in reviewing credible-fear applications.

The three key pieces of U.S. border security and immigration enforcement are not reflective of the violent conditions in Mexico. Rather, they reflect a paradigm in which international terrorism set the security agenda for the border, and illegal Mexican migration set the conditions for crossing it. The escalation in border security has "translated into tougher laws, rising budgets and agency growth, the deployment of more sophisticated equipment and surveillance technologies, and a growing fusion between law enforcement and national security institutions and missions."[47] The case of narco-refugees challenges this current understanding, and a steady or sudden increase in their numbers may very well shatter the prevailing paradigm of security and migration.

"MEXI-STAN": WHAT COULD BE

Having a "war zone" next door should force policymakers to do some new thinking about the relationship between security and migration. Based on recent events, the levels of violence are increasing, while its scope is expanding:

- In 2010, over a dozen mayors were killed, including one in City Hall.
- January 31, 2010—Suspected cartel hitmen killed 13 high school students and two adults at a party in Ciudad Juarez.
- March 28, 2010—Gunmen in northwestern Durango state killed 10 people, some as young as 8 years old, after the pick-up truck they were traveling in sped through a roadblock on an isolated highway in the drug-producing "Golden Triangle" region.
- June 11, 2010—Two dozen heavily armed gunmen burst into a drug rehabilitation clinic in the northern state of Chihuahua and killed 19 addicts, ranging in age from 18 to 25.
- June 28, 2010—Suspected cartel hitmen shot and killed a popular gubernatorial candidate in the northern state of Tamaulipas.

- July 15, 2010—A 22-pound (10-kilo) car bomb killed four people in Ciudad Juarez in a blast detonated by cell phone, the first such attack since Calderon took office.
- July 18, 2010—Gunmen burst into a birthday party in the northern city of Torreon, using automatic weapons to kill 17 party-goers and wound 18 others. Mexican authorities later said those responsible were incarcerated cartel hit-men who were let out of jail by corrupt officials. The killers allegedly borrowed weapons and vehicles from prison guards and later returned to their cells.
- August 18, 2010—The body of the mayor of Santiago, a colonial tourist town near Monterrey, was dumped on a rural road 2 days after he was taken from his home.
- August 24, 2010—Los Zetas massacred 72 migrants who refused to work for them. The two lead investigators of the massacre were found dead 3 days later.[48]

From the nature of such violence, we can imagine three dire scenarios that would force the narco-refugee issue onto the national policymaking agenda. One scenario is the "new normal," meaning that the current violence leads to a mutually reinforcing instability between Mexico and the United States. In this scenario, drug violence in the United States and Mexico will become a fact of life in relations between the two countries. Drug gang and cartel violence will seep into the United States along with the supply of drugs. Flare-ups in violence will be followed by periods of calm, only to be followed by the return of familiar patterns of killings and mutilations. This scenario would likely result in a slow but steady increase in the numbers of narco-refugees coming to the United States. Pressures from many quarters of the American public for more adequate responses would come to bear — on one side would be those seeking more expeditious procedures for accepting Mexicans caught in the crossfire of the violence, while the other side would likely favor either continuing the current asylum process or tightening it against future surges of narco-refugees.

The second scenario could be an "accidental narco" syndrome developing in Mexico. Unlike the balloon effect of counternarcotics operations, which causes the shift of trafficking to other regions, and unlike David Kilcullen's notion of the "accidental guerrilla," whereby pursuit of jihadist terror groups only leads to the creation of more insurgents, the accidental narco refers to the Mexican government becoming a type of cartel enforcer in its own right. Tempted to show progress to the United States and the Mexican people in lowering drug violence, the Mexican government may choose to collude with some of the less violent cartels to gain intelligence and information to use against the most violent ones.

In essence, the government becomes an armed wing of the cooperative cartels by clamping down on rivals and arresting its members. Depending on the scope and intensity of the Mexican state's actions, violence could increase in the near term or become protracted, depending on the capabilities and will of the targeted cartels. There has been a glimpse of this phenomenon with the car bomb detonated in July 2010. Graffiti on a wall of a shopping mall claimed responsibility for the car bomb used against Mexican law enforcement; it read in Spanish: "What happened on the 16 (street) is going to keep happening to all the authorities that continue to support Chapo (Guzman). Sincerely, the Juarez Cartel. We still have car bombs (expletive), ha, ha."[49]

Another message aimed at the Federal Bureau of Investigation (FBI) and DEA was posted in an elementary school in Juarez: "FBI and DEA, start investigating authorities that support the Sinaloa Cartel, if you do not, we will get those federal officers with car bombs. If corrupt federal officers are not arrested within 15 days, we will put 100 kilograms of C-4 in a car."[50] Under an accidental narco scenario, there could be a sharp increase in the number of narco-refugees, as violence intensifies and escalates due to last-ditch efforts by cartels to prevent defeat. U.S. policymakers may have to adjust rapidly to accommodate larger numbers of Mexicans fleeing their country. However, if the government's approach works in the short term, there may be fewer narco-refugees. If the government succeeds, but only after a protracted campaign, peace may return to Mexico, which would be conducive to a cautious repatriation process.

The third imaginable scenario is that a "Zeta state" might emerge. This does not mean the collapse of the Mexican state and the replacement by the Zetas. Rather, the Zetas and other violent actors may evolve (or devolve) into militias or warlord fiefdoms alongside the proliferation of private security firms hired by wealthier Mexicans to protect themselves from drug violence. A type of shadow state may emerge, with these groups drawing more and more legitimacy away from the Mexican state, which will be viewed as increasingly powerless to curb lawlessness. Depending on what happens with the cartels, violence may increase with the number of additional players, or a type of balance of power may emerge. This scenario, in turn, may become a type of "new normal," with the attendant pressures on policymakers as described above.

These three potential scenarios lead to an important caveat—none is mutually exclusive, nor would each scenario need to apply to the entire country of Mexico. States may find pockets of these conditions, with particular cities and towns being compromised. Mexico may or may not be on its way to becoming a "narco-state," but there are several "narco-cities" in Mexico. President Felipe Calderon has referred to them as "zones of impunity." A number of narco-cities strung together or an increase in their number would lead to an expansion of the zones of impunity, weakening the overall health of the Mexican state and likely leading to the creation of more narco-refugees.

It is just as significant to consider what might be some warning signs of a turn for the worse toward fulfillment of these potential scenarios. First, while several members of police departments have sought safety in the United States, no members of the Mexican military have done so. If there were a noticeable trend among Mexican military members toward becoming narco-refugees, it would mean that the most coercive arm of the state does not believe that it can prevail against the cartels, nor do its members feel that they were safe from personal reprisals. Similarly, if the Mexican military merely returns to barracks and refuses to participate in any future campaigns against the cartels, then this, too, would be a decidedly negative indication. Ominously, the revenge killings of the family of the Mexican marine who shot and killed one of the leaders of the Beltran-Leyva organization speaks to the power of the cartels to reach out and inflict pain on select members of the Mexican security apparatus. The open question is whether they could do so on a much wider scale.

Second, an increasing exodus of educated and prosperous Mexicans would also indicate that the security situation continues to be poor or is deteriorating. Currently, the business shakedowns for protection; kidnapping businessmen and professionals for ransom; along with murder-for-hire schemes; occur with or without any linkages to the drug trade. These activities act as stand-alone profit-making activities equivalent to "a parallel tax system that threatens the government monopoly on raising tax money."[51] The significant pay received by gangs acts as an incentive perpetuating the occurrence of violence.[52] In a country with significant disparities in wealth, these activities are likely to be continued, meaning more middle-class Mexicans may decide to leave their country. "One young Mexican executive at cement giant Cemex SAB, which has headquarters in Monterrey, said he can count at least 20 different families from his circle of friends who have left—nearly all of them for nearby Texas."[53] Such an exodus, including the inherent brain drain, may also affect the Mexican economy.

Reduced U.S. investment may be a third worrisome indicator. A sudden economic decline in Mexico related to drug violence will also affect the United States. There are some haunting indications from the city of Monterrey. Known as the "Sultan of the North," it is a wealthy city that is home to a number of Mexican companies and American subsidiaries. Monterrey has not been immune from drug violence, even though it is 4 hours from the border. According to the director of Altegrity Risk International, "U.S. companies see Monterrey as high-risk right now."[54] Tourism in the city is down, which has compounded the sluggish economic recovery following the recession. The U.S. Chamber of Commerce in Mexico surveyed its members countrywide and found that *a quarter* of them were reconsidering their investments in Mexico as a result of worries over security; 16 percent of them suffered extortion; and 13 percent experienced kidnappings.[55] Several large companies have decided not to invest in Mexico because of the drug violence; among them are Electrolux and Whirlpool.[56] In the estimation of J.P. Morgan's chief economist for Mexico, the country likely lost approximately $4 billion in investment in 2010 when companies reconsidered such plans because of drug violence.[57]

But many small businesses in Mexico are also at the mercy of the violence. They are subject to extortion by cartels and gangs, while facing a drop in revenue due to a decrease in tourism.[58] In Ciudad Juarez, more than 2,500 small grocery stores have closed due to extortion or because customers have left the city; the Mexican social security administration believes that 75,000 residents there have lost their jobs since 2007.[59] Without relief, business owners may also become part of the exodus to the United States. When key businesses close, customers who depend on their services also begin to move. In Ciudad Mier, medical services were affected by cartel violence. Pharmacies were closing, and the pharmaceutical reserves in town began to vanish when delivery drivers were unable to safely travel the highway, fearing they would be attacked during their journey.[60] Oil fields and cropland have also been abandoned in some areas out of fear of being in the crossfire of cartels and gangs. In the Burgos Basin, site of Mexico's biggest natural gas field in the state of Tamaulipas, gunmen seized the Gigante Uno gas plant and kidnapped five Pemex workers.

According to a recent press release from the Mexican Senate, "The unsafe conditions are preventing Pemex from extracting 150 million cubic meters of natural gas in the Burgos Basin."[61] In Tamaulipas, it is estimated that about 5,000 ranches may have been abandoned, according to the Tamaulipas Regional Ranchers Association, or URGT. "The industry has been losing money, and exports of young bulls to the United States have fallen considerably, [the head of URGT] said. Some 200,000 head of cattle were exported in 2009, but exports will only reach about one-third of that level this year."[62] A steep economic decline may create compounding effects. The number of illegal immigrants to the United States who are not searching for safety necessarily but are searching for employment may increase. In addition, a poor employment situation may swell the ranks of gangs and cartels, creating even greater disorder.

A fourth worrying sign would be significant violence aimed at national politicians in Mexico during the elections in 2012. The trend in assassinations and attempted assassinations is not reassuring. In 2008, 11 men were arrested and accused of planning a high-level assassination with the possible collaboration of Mexico City police and former army soldiers.[63] The bulk of cartel assassinations of governmental figures has been limited to police officers and mayors, but a leading politician who was almost certain to win the governorship of the northern state of Tamaulipas was assassinated just days before the election. He pledged to be tougher on organized crime than his predecessor. With the kidnapping of former presidential candidate Diego Fernandez de Cevallos, a power broker in Calderon's ruling National Action Party (PAN), the possibility of more visible displays of violence directed at higher-profile national politicians cannot be discounted. Shockingly, in late 2008, a major in the Mexican army who was part of President Calderon's personal security detail was arrested for being on the payroll of the Beltran-Leyva cartel. He is believed to have passed along information regarding the activities and travel plans of the Mexican president.[64]

Finally, another warning sign would be the morphing of the capital, Mexico City, into a zone of insecurity. The heart of any nation is its capital. If the heartbeat finds itself at the mercy of civil violence, the health of the rest of country is put in jeopardy. Citizens begin to question the very legitimacy, authority, and capacity of the state to meet their most fundamental needs. In instances of civil violence in the capitals of other countries, many citizens have moved toward safety or taken actions to secure themselves. This reaction has meant additional violence, which led to an even greater exodus. Mexico City has been plagued with high levels of street crime and police corruption, but it has been relatively immune from the types of violence that has gripped border cities. The capital has been largely a place of peace, where high-level drug traffickers coexisted with each other and the government. But now, with a more confrontational stance taken by the parties, a number of senior drug cartel members have been arrested or killed near the capital. The sons of Sinaloa and Gulf cartels were caught in the upscale suburbs of Mexico City; Edgar Valdez Villareal of the Beltran-Leyva organization was caught in Morelos near Mexico City; and Arturo Beltran-Leyva was killed in a town in the state of Morelos. Cartel violence has also been slowly inching toward the capital. In 2008 alone, three senior law enforcement officials were assassinated: Roberto Bravo, Director of

Investigations of the Sensitive Investigations Unit of the Federal police; Edgar Gomez, General Coordinator for Regional Security at the Mexican Secretariat of Public Security; and Igor Calderon of the Federal Investigative Agency. In the same year, the editor of *El Real* newspaper was shot to death as he drove in a Mexico City suburb. In Cuernavaca, four decapitated men were hung from a bridge in August 2010. Cuernavaca is a favorite destination for residents of Mexico City, which is just over 50 miles away. Conversion of Mexico City into a battleground is not out of the realm of the possible if cartels and their enforcers feel that the government is giving them no choice but to strike deep into the heart of the state's power.

"Waziristan, USA": Effects in the United States.

There will be some potentially chilling effects if the number of narco-refugees to the United States increases dramatically, no matter under what scenario or conditions. The product might be what Nate Freier terms "strategic shock," whereby:

> The unanticipated onset forces the entire defense enterprise to reorient and restructure institutions, employ capabilities in unexpected ways, and confront challenges that are fundamentally different than those routinely considered in defense calculations. . . . The likeliest and most dangerous future shocks will be unconventional. They will not emerge from thunderbolt advances in an opponent's military capabilities. Rather, they will manifest themselves in ways far outside established defense convention. Most will be nonmilitary in origin and character, and not, by definition, defense-specific events conducive to the conventional employment of the [Department of Defense] enterprise. . . . They will rise from an analytical no man's

land separating well-considered . . . defense contingencies and pure defense speculation. Their origin is most likely to be in irregular, catastrophic, and hybrid threats of "purpose" (emerging from hostile design) or threats of "context" (emerging in the absence of hostile purpose or design). Of the two, the latter is both the least understood and the most dangerous.[65]

Narco-refugees may be a strategic shock, a "threat of context," but they may also foreshadow potentially greater shocks for U.S. policymakers to tackle. Such shocks will mirror what other large refugee waves have created in other countries, but will have features unique to the U.S.-Mexico relationship.

Like many refugee waves in other places, grievances from the country in conflict can transfer to the host country. In the context of narco-refugees, the battlefields of Mexican cartel violence may shift to the United States in ways previously not experienced. Once again, this would be due to geographic proximity. The "heartland" or core of criminal power for Mexican drug cartels is composed of six Mexican states that border the United States and contain the *plazas*: Baja California, Sonora, Chihuahua, Coahuila, Nuevo Leon, and Tamaulipas. The adjacent U.S. states of California, Arizona, New Mexico, and Texas will likely experience the greatest influx of narco-refugees from neighboring heartland states. These Mexican and U.S. states, which share the border, may form a zone of instability, similar to Waziristan in northwest Pakistan. Not all refugees are benign, and the longer that they remain outside of their home country and without adequate employment, the greater the likelihood of narco-refugees using the United States as a safe haven for violent operations southbound. Beyond just revenge killings, vigilante squads may form to return to Mexico in an attempt to clear towns of cartels and gangs. With easy access to guns in the United States, these squads could potentially conduct operations to establish conditions for the return of narco-refugees to Mexico. The question is whether the U.S. Government would seek to prevent or support such actions and what role the Department of Defense (DoD) or DHS would play in such a scenario.

While the idea of U.S. border states serving as a safe haven for violent raids against cartels and gangs in Mexico may seem far-fetched at the moment, there are a number of elements that lend themselves to the plausibility of such a development. It is important to keep in mind that one of the most brutal cartels—the one that began the campaign of beheadings—is La Familia Michoacana (LFM), which is believed to have started as a vigilante group to combat drug dealers and kidnappers. LFM has committed acts of violence in the United States to punish rivals in the United States and Mexico. Although not as sophisticated as LFM, lynch mobs have formed in Mexico and have acted against suspected kidnappers. In one instance, a mob blocked federal police from intervening to stop the beating of two suspected gang members.[66] Far more ominously, armed groups have sprouted up in several Mexican states. The Citizens' Command for Juarez, financed by local businessmen, promises to "end a criminal's life every 24 hours" and considers itself to be the "first citizens' post-revolutionary movement"; the Popular Anti-Drug Army has been hanging banners in various cities in Guerrero and Morelos challenging the cartels; a rancher in Guerrero formed a group called the Army that Liberates the People and has hung banners with messages that threaten the region's drug traffickers, as well as praising the Mexican military "for its achievements in the struggle against drug trafficking."[67] As one expert on organized crime states, "The paramilitary model in Mexico is different from Colombia. In Colombia irregular troops are organized to take over territory, houses, etc. In Mexico, paramilitary communities are created. They infiltrate them, they prepare them, and then become paramilitary communities."[68] There would be little to stop such paramilitary communities from cropping up in the United States with the right mixture.

Part of the mixture already exists. The cases of Mexican mayors who reside in the United States demonstrate the ability to use the United States as a safe haven and to continue to make decisions from afar. "The advantage for them is that they cross the Rio Bravo (Rio Grande), and they are in their city hall or their home . . . or govern with the telephone in their hand."[69] The current use of B1/B2 visas by *inversionistas* has also been mimicked by reputed gang and cartel members.

> Traditionally, when violence has spiked in Mexico, cartel figures have used U.S. cities such as Laredo, El Paso and San Diego as rest and recreation spots, reasoning that the general umbrella of safety provided by U.S. law enforcement to those residing in the United States would protect them from assassination by their enemies. As bolder Mexican cartel hit men have begun to carry out assassinations on the U.S. side of the border in places such as Laredo, Rio Bravo, and even Dallas, the cartel figures have begun to seek sanctuary even deeper in the United States, thereby bringing the threat with them.[70]

Such an umbrella of protection can be used by Mexicans who seek to organize themselves in groups to forcibly return to Mexico. However, these groups would also be subject to attacks in the United States by cartels and gangs who seek to prevent them from interfering in their illicit operations.

Paths to be Considered.

The current paradigm of security and migration has, in part, been the product of the decades-long War on Drugs. As Ryan Brim, author of *This is Your Country on Drugs*, puts it:

> In reality, there is no such thing as drug policy. As currently understood and implemented, drug policy attempts to isolate a phenomenon that can't be taken in isolation. Economic policy is drug policy. Health-care is drug policy. Foreign policy, too, is drug policy. When approached in isolation, drug policy almost always backfires because it doesn't take into account powerful economic, social and cultural forces.[71]

Increasingly, when looking at Mexico and the phenomenon of narco-refugees, drug policy cannot be divorced from immigration policy or national security, and yet the effects of narco-refugees in the United States may shatter this paradigm as well. Americans spend between $18 billion and $39 billion annually on narcotics coming northward.[72] As former Mexican Attorney General Eduardo Medina Mora stated, "In that sense, the U.S. is already financing this war. It is just financing the wrong side."[73] Drug profits are in the same range as or outstrip many areas of the legitimate commerce between the two nations, such as annual remittances southbound from the Mexican community in the United States which total $23 billion,[74] while the revenues generated by the Mexican tourism industry before the recession totaled nearly $11 billion.[75] In contrast, the United States has spent more than $2.5 trillion over the past 40 years in the War on Drugs, yet drug use has remained constant, with ebbs and flows based on shifts in the types of drugs consumed. As long as this demand continues, there is a high likelihood that cartel violence will as well.

With as little fanfare as there was outrage, Gil Kerlikowske, Director of the U.S. Office of National Drug Control Policy (the "Drug Czar"), scrapped the phrase "the War on Drugs" and sought to redirect efforts to achieve reduction of drug use. This was not a step toward legalization or decriminalization. A considerable proportion of the federal counternarcotics budget is still aimed at supply-side reduction, interdiction, and law enforcement. Prohibition is still the overarching framework under which drug demand is to be tackled in the United States. But short of a near 180-degree turn in drug consumption in the United States, illegal profits will continue to flow into the pockets of the drug cartels, meaning that gangs and enforcer groups will foment the conditions in Mexico for narco-refugees.

There are a number of policy options for dealing with the current numbers, or a steady rise in numbers, of Mexican asylum cases. Each of these options would have to be tied to an overall assessment of what is going on in Mexico. Insurgency or criminality would make the various paths for asylum more logical than others or require significant adjustments to the current way that the United States handles asylum cases in general. There are three broad frameworks that can be considered: the zigzag path, broad path, and narrow path.

The zigzag path would follow the current trend of allowing Mexican state agents like political leaders, members of security forces, and important members of civil society, such as journalists, to have greater access to the United States. A special temporary visa could be granted to individuals in these categories. However, the potential downside is the message that it sends to Mexican policymakers and U.S. investors: Mexico is very unsafe for key people of the country and could be that way for an extended period. This policy would also exclude a number of Mexicans who are still threatened by the cartels, but do not have key positions in government or in the community.

The broad path would seek legislation or policy prescriptions to broaden the legal definition of "refugee" so as to include those whose motive is to escape criminal violence. This step would increase the clarity and efficiency of the immigration process when dealing with narco-refugees. It would also allow for a greater number of Mexicans to qualify for asylum, even if they are not state agents or prominent members of their communities. Such a path may be narrowed slightly by offering sanctuary to those Mexicans who have American relatives willing to serve as sponsors. However, such a criterion might allow a number of individuals from other countries to claim this status, thereby increasing the need for additional program resources or creating additional inefficiency.

The narrow path would emphasize a more stringent process for Mexican asylum seekers. This approach would increase the difficulty by reinstating detention and limiting access to LAPR cards for those seeking asylum. Credible-fear interviews would be more thorough in their vetting in order to avoid potential abuses. With more thorough background investigations, the possibility of limiting the numbers might also reduce the likelihood of "Waziristan, USA" coming to fruition. However, to clamp down more stringently might increase illegal immigration, as asylum seekers attempt to circumvent the cumbersome process for entering the United States legally.

There are no objective criteria for deciding which policy must be implemented. The timing of any change in policy must also be considered. Any path could be settled on now, including retention of the status quo. Policymakers may gradually come to determine what path asylum seekers would take as time unfolds. Making an immediate change in policy without an overall assessment of the situation in Mexico, and taking into account the great desirability of a stable and positive U.S.-Mexico relationship, might be folly. A change could be made based on such conditions as a steady but rising number of narco-refugees or intermittent surges in numbers. Policymakers may also want to consider a triggered response to any changes in Mexico that portend truly calamitous consequences for either country. Once again, those seeking asylum may be an omen of changes in the health of the Mexican state, e.g., a rise in the numbers of certain types of key individuals: military members, federal politicians, and prominent business leaders.

A *sudden* mass exodus, however, would pose special problems. Any policy option and the timing of its implementation would be subject to a number of questions demanding answers. Would the sheer volume of people in a short period of time require U.S. detention facilities where Mexicans would be held as the determination of their status unfolds? Would they be allowed into the United States on special visas and under stipulated restrictions (for example, that they not travel farther than 25 miles north of the border and may not seek employment)? Would U.S. sponsors be allowed to host Mexicans in certain cases? For those who are permitted to remain in the United States, would they be issued LAPR cards, as the current policy allows? Finally, what conditions in Mexico would be favorable for narco-refugees to be repatriated when the violence subsides? Policymakers should be prepared to answer these questions, politically charged as they are, *before* any sudden wave of narco-refugees moves towards the U.S. border.

BORDER, FRONTIER, LINE . . . SANCTUARY

It would be a mistake to predict that all hope for Mexico is lost and that the United States will be subject to a rising tide or sudden tsunami of narco-refugees. The Mexican government may yet prevail in its war against the cartels, and the United States may avoid a strategic shock. Yet, the displacement of Mexicans may well create a disturbance of U.S. strategic priorities. For U.S. policymakers confronted with such a reality, there may not be a credible border, frontier, or line to serve as a protective obstacle when the issues surrounding narco-refugees become ever more pressing, ever more immediate. By beginning the process of deliberation on these issues now, finding an acceptable strategic sanctuary for the refugees in the future becomes a possibility.

ENDNOTES

1. James McKinley, Jr., "Fleeing Drug Violence, Mexicans Pour into the US," *New York Times*, April 17, 2010, available from *www.nytimes.com/2010/04/18/us/18border.html?pagewanted=1&hp*.

2. Philip Sherwell, "Mexican Drug Wars Force Police to Claim Asylum in US," *The Daily Telegraph*, April 11, 2009, available from *www.telegraph.co.uk*.

3. *Ibid.*; Alfonso Chardy, "Mexicans Caught in Drug War get US Asylum," April 5, 2010, available from *www.azcentral.com.*

4. William Booth, "US Agents to Fight Drug Cartels in Mexico," *msnbc.com*, February 24, 2010, available from *msnbc.msn.com/ id/35556681/ns/world_news-washington_post/.*

5. "Over 200,000 Leave Mexico Border City," *Latin America Herald Tribune*, October 14, 2010, available from *www.laht.com/ article.asp?ArticleId=367604&CategoryId=14091.*

6. Jason Beaubien, "In Just One Year, A Mexican City Turns Violent," *NPR.org*, October 16, 2010, available from *www.npr.org/ templates/story/story.php?storyId=130592600.*

7. See, for example, "Immigrants Crossing into Arizona on the Rise," *www.msnbc.com*, May 18, 2010, available from *www. msnbc.msn.com/id/37214634/.*

8. Antonio Castelan, "Drug Cartel Members Kidnapping People in San Diego County," October 9, 2009, available from *www. sandiego6.com.*

9. Jorge Chabat quoted in William Booth, "Mexican Cartels Send Messages of Death," *www.msnbc.com*, December 4, 2008, available from *www.msnbc.com/id/2804515/print/1/ displaymode/1098.*

10. Tony Payan, *The Three US-Mexico Border Wars*, Westport, CT: Praeger Security International, 2006, p. 20.

11. Luz Nagle, "Corruption of Politicians, Law Enforcement, and the Judiciary in Mexico and Complicity Across the Border," *Small Wars and Insurgencies*, March 2010, p. 95.

12. Charles Bowden and Alice Leora Briggs, *Dreamland: The Way Out of Juarez*, Austin, TX: University of Texas Press, 2010, p. 6.

13. Paul Rexton Kan and Phil Williams, "Afterword: Criminal Violence in Mexico — A Dissenting Analysis," *Small Wars and Insurgencies*, March 2010, p. 221.

14. *Ibid.*, 223.

15. KBPS, "Border Battle: Bringing Home the Drug War, Glossary," available from *www.kpbs.org/news/border-battle/*.

16. James Rule, *Theories of Civil Violence*, Los Angeles, CA: University of California Press, 1988, p. 2.

17. Barry McCaffrey, "After Action Report – VISIT MEXICO – 5–7 December 2008," p. 4.

18. Hal Brands, *Mexico's Narco-Insurgency and US Counterdrug Policy*, Carlisle, PA: Strategic Studies Institute, U.S. Army War College, May 2009, pp. 4-5.

19. Adam Entous and Nathan Hodge, "US Sees Heightened Threat in Mexico," *Wall Street Journal*, September 10, 2010, p. 8.

20. Kan and Williams, "Afterword," p. 221.

21. Robert Bunker and John Sullivan, "Cartel Evolution Revisted: Third Phase Cartel Potential and Alternative Futures in Mexico," *Small Wars and Insurgencies*, March 2010, p. 30.

22. Brands, p. 11.

23. Hiram Soto, "Kidnappings are Driving Baja Citizens to County," August 30, 2008, available from *www.signonsandiego*.

24. See *www.puertasmultilock.com*.

25. David Luhnow and Jose de Cordoba, "The Perilous State of Mexico," *The Wall Street Journal Online*, February 21, 2009, available from *online.wsj.com/article/SB123518102536038463.html*.

26. *Ibid.*

27. "Por que se fue Alejandro Junco" ("Why Alejandro Junco Left), *Reporte Indigo*, September 12, 2008, *www.reporteindigo.com*, available from *octavioislas.wordpress.com/2008/09/13/1732-mexico-reporte-indigo-12-de-septiembre-de-2008-nuevo-periodismo-digital-en-mexico/*.

28. "Threats from Narcos Force Mayors to Live in US," *borderlandbeat.com*, September 27, 2010, available from *www.border landbeat.com/2010/09/threats-from-narcos-force-mexican.html*.

29. 1951 Refugee Convention Ratified by the United States in the Immigration and Nationality Act (INA) Section 101(a)(42)(A).

30. Thanks are due to Tom Boerman for providing the details on asylum proceedings.

31. Daniel Gonzalez, "More Fleeing Cartels in Mexico, Seeking Asylum in US," *The Arizona Republic*, January 24, 2010, available from *www.azcentral.com/news/articles/2010/01/24/20100124asyl um0124.html*.

32. *Ibid.*

33. McKinley.

34. Bob Grotenhuis, "Cartel Strengthens Hold on Juarez Valley," *www.ktsm.com*, April 17, 2010, available from *www.ktsm.com/news/cartel-strengthens-hold-on-juarez-valley*.

35. Adriana Chavez, "'I'm scared for my life': Televisa cameraman seeks asylum in the US," *El Paso Times*, September 15, 2010, available from *www.elpasotimes.com/news/ci_16077238?IADID=Search-www.elpasotimes.com-www.elpasotimes.com*.

36. Maria de la Luz Gonzales (2009-03-25), "Suman 10 mil 475 ejecuciones en esta administracion: PGR" (A Total of 10,475 executions in this administration: PGR), in Spanish, *El Universal*, available from *www.eluniversal.com.mx/nacion/166613.html*.

37. Colin Peters, "Americas Overview," Vienna, Austria: International Press Institute, February 9, 2010, available from *www.freemedia.at/publications/world-press-freedom-review/americas-carribean/singleview/4729/*.

38. Sherwell.

39. Ed Barnes, "Mexicans Facing Drug War Violence Could Seek Political Asylum in US," *www.foxnews.com*, April 1, 2010, available from *www.foxnews.com/us/2010/04/01/mexicans-facing-drug-war-violence-seek-political-asylum/*.

40. *Ibid.*

41. Sara Carter, "Ex-Officer Fights Deportation, Death"*www.washingtontimes.com*, March 10, 2009, available from *www.washingtontimes.com/news/2009/mar/10/ex-officer-fights-deportation-death/*.

42. Susan Ginsburg, *Security and Human Mobility in an Age of Risk*, Washington, DC: Migration Policy Institute, 2010, p. 7.

43. Tracy Wilkinson, "Under Threat from Mexican Drug Cartels, Reporters go Silent," *Los Angeles Times*, August 16, 2010, available from *www.latimes.com/news/nationworld/world/la-fg-mexico-narco-censorship-20100816,0,4152944.story*.

44. Chavez.

45. Lisa J. Campbell, "Los Zetas: An Operational Assessment," *Small Wars & Insurgencies*, March 2010, p. 67.

46. "Que quieren de nosotros?" *El Diario de Juarez*, September 20, 2010, available from *www.diario.com.mx/notas.php?f=2010/09/19&id=ce557112f34b187454d7b6d117a76cb5*.

47. Peter Andreas, *Border Games*, Ithaca, NY: Cornell University Press, 2009, p. 4.

48. "Factbox: Worst Attacks in Mexico's Drug War," compiled by *www.borderlandbeat.com*, August 20, 2010.

49. Alicia Caldwell, "US Official: Mexican Car Bomb Likely Used Tovex," *Washington Post*, July 19, 2010, available from *www.washingtonpost.com/wp-dyn/content/article/2010/07/19/AR2010071901027.html*.

50. Foreign Military Studies Office, Latin America Security Watch, "Mexico: Special Interest," July 19, 2010. Spanish source available from *www.elagoradechihuahua.com/Amenazan-con-mas-coches-bomba,25606.html*.

51. David Luhnow and Jose de Cordoba, "The Perilous State of Mexico," *The Wall Street Journal Online*, February 21, 2009, available from *online.wsj.com/article/SB123518102536038463.html*.

52. Pamela Bunker, Lisa Campbell, and Robert Bunker, "Torture, Beheadings, and Narcocultos," *Small Wars & Insurgencies*, March 2010, p. 150.

53. David Luhnow, "Elites Flees Drug War in Mexico's No. 3 City," *Wall Street Journal*, September 10, 2010, available from *online.wsj.com/article/SB100014240527487046444045754825734385565 34.html*.

54. Nicholas Casey, "Mexico Under Seige," *Wall Street Journal*, August 19, 2010, aavailable from *online.wsj.com/article/SB10001424 0527487045577045754377626462092 70.html*.

55. "A One-Two Punch," *The Economist*, May 29, 2010, p. 40.

56. Nicholas Casey and James Hagerty, "Companies Shun Violent Mexico," *Wall Street Journal*, December 17, 2010, available from *online.wsj.com/article/SB10001424052748703395204576023811 983098994.html?mod=WSJ_hp_MIDDLENexttoWhatsNewsTop*.

57. *Ibid*.

58. "Mexico: The Struggle for Balance," *STRATFOR*, April 8, 2010, available from *www.stratfor.com/weekly/20100407_mexico_struggle_balance*.

59. Booth, *msnbc.com*.

60. Nicholas Casey and Jose de Codoba, "Northern Mexico's State of Anarchy," *Wall Street Journal*, November 20-21, 2010, p. A13.

61. David Agren, "Oil: The Mexican Cartels' Other Deadly Business," *The Globe and Mail*, December 21, 2010, available from *www.theglobeandmail.com/news/world/americas/oil-the-mexican-cartels-other-deadly-business/article1845378/*.

62. "Thousands of Ranches Abandoned in Tamaulipas Due to Violence," *borderlandbeat*, November 27, 2010, available from *www.borderlandbeat.com/2010/11/thousands-of-ranches-abandoned-in.html*.

63. Laurence Iliff and Alfredo Corchado, "Drug Violence Has Moved Into Mexico City," *Dallas Morning News*, February 8, 2008, available from *www.dallasnews.com/sharedcontent/dws/news/texas-southwest/stories/DN-capital_08int.ART.North.Edition1.45119ad.html*.

64. *STRATFOR, Mexico in Crisis,* Austin, TX: STRATFOR, 2009, p. 184.

65. Nathan Freier, *Known Unknowns: Strategic Shocks in Defense Strategy Development*, Carlisle, PA: Strategic Studies Institute, U.S. Army War College, 2008, pp. 11-15.

66. Nacha Cattan, "Fed Up with Plague of Kidnappings, Mexicans Turn to Mob Justice," *Christian Science Monitor*, September 22, 2010, available from *www.csmonitor.com/World/Americas/2010/0922/Fed-up-with-plague-of-kidnappings-Mexicans-turn-to-mob-justice*.

67. Diego Enrique Osorno, "Vigilante Groups Appear in Five Mexican States," *El Milenio*, January 26, 2009, available from *narcosphere.narconews.com/notebook/kristin-bricker/2009/01/vigilante-groups-appear-five-mexican-states*.

68. *Ibid.*

69. "Threats from Narcos Force Mayors to Live in US," *borderlandbeat.com*.

70. *STRATFOR, Mexico in Crisis*, p. 96.

71. Ryan Grim, *This is Your Country on Drugs*, Hoboken, NJ: Wiley and Sons, 2009, p. 16.

72. Andrew Selee, David Shirk, and Eric Olson, "Five Myths about Mexico's Drug War," *The Washington Post*, March 28, 2010, p. B3.

73. Mark Potter, "Drug War 'Alarming' US Officials," *msnbc.com*, June 25, 2008, available from *worldblog.msnbc.msn.com/archive/2008/06/25/1166487.aspx*.

74. Sarah Miller Llana, "Mexican Workers Send Less Cash Home from US," *Christian Science Monitor*, January 28, 2009, available from *www.csmonitor.com/World/Americas/2009/0128/p25s20-woam.html*.

75. Secretario de Turismo, Mexico, March 7, 2007, available from *www.1888pressrelease.com/mexico-s-international-tourism-revenues-reach-historic-high-pr-8r82w4eo15.html*.